7 Waste Observation Worksheet

DEFECTS

INVENTORY

PROCESSING

WAITING

MOTION

TRANSPORTATION

OVERPRODUCTION

7 Wastes Observation Worksheet

DEFECTS

INVENTORY

PROCESSING

WAITING

MOTION

TRANSPORTATION

OVERPRODUCTION

7 Wastes Observation Worksheet

DEFECTS

INVENTORY

PROCESSING

WAITING

MOTION

TRANSPORTATION

OVERPRODUCTION

ENNA
KNOWLEDGE INTO PRACTICE

www.enna.com

7 Waste Observation Worksheet

DEFECTS

INVENTORY

PROCESSING

WAITING

MOTION

TRANSPORTATION

OVERPRODUCTION

ENNA
KNOWLEDGE INTO PRACTICE

www.enna.com

7 Waste Observation Worksheet

DEFECTS

INVENTORY

PROCESSING

WAITING

MOTION

TRANSPORTATION

OVERPRODUCTION

ENNA
KNOWLEDGE INTO PRACTICE

7 Wastes Observation Worksheet

DEFECTS

INVENTORY

PROCESSING

WAITING

MOTION

TRANSPORTATION

OVERPRODUCTION

ENNA
KNOWLEDGE INTO PRACTICE

7 Wastes Observation Worksheet

DEFECTS

INVENTORY

PROCESSING

WAITING

MOTION

TRANSPORTATION

OVERPRODUCTION

7 Wastes Observation Worksheet

DEFECTS

INVENTORY

PROCESSING

WAITING

MOTION

TRANSPORTATION

OVERPRODUCTION

7 Wastes Observation Worksheet

DEFECTS

INVENTORY

PROCESSING

WAITING

MOTION

TRANSPORTATION

OVERPRODUCTION

KNOWLEDGE INTO PRACTICE

www.enna.com

7 Wastes Observation Worksheet

DEFECTS

INVENTORY

PROCESSING

WAITING

MOTION

TRANSPORTATION

OVERPRODUCTION

7 Wastes Observation Worksheet

DEFECTS

INVENTORY

PROCESSING

WAITING

MOTION

TRANSPORTATION

OVERPRODUCTION

7 Wastes Observation Worksheet

DEFECTS

INVENTORY

PROCESSING

WAITING

MOTION

TRANSPORTATION

OVERPRODUCTION

7 Wastes Observation Worksheet

DEFECTS

INVENTORY

PROCESSING

WAITING

MOTION

TRANSPORTATION

OVERPRODUCTION

KNOWLEDGE INTO PRACTICE

www.enna.com

7 Wastes Observation Worksheet

DEFECTS

INVENTORY

PROCESSING

WAITING

MOTION

TRANSPORTATION

OVERPRODUCTION

7 Wastes Observation Worksheet

DEFECTS

INVENTORY

PROCESSING

WAITING

MOTION

TRANSPORTATION

OVERPRODUCTION

KNOWLEDGE INTO PRACTICE

www.enna.com

7 Wastes Observation Worksheet

DEFECTS

INVENTORY

PROCESSING

WAITING

MOTION

TRANSPORTATION

OVERPRODUCTION

ENNA
KNOWLEDGE INTO PRACTICE

7 Wastes Observation Worksheet

DEFECTS

INVENTORY

PROCESSING

WAITING

MOTION

TRANSPORTATION

OVERPRODUCTION

7 Waste Observation Worksheet

DEFECTS

INVENTORY

PROCESSING

WAITING

MOTION

TRANSPORTATION

OVERPRODUCTION

7 Wastes Observation Worksheet

DEFECTS

INVENTORY

PROCESSING

WAITING

MOTION

TRANSPORTATION

OVERPRODUCTION

7 Wastes Observation Worksheet

DEFECTS

INVENTORY

PROCESSING

WAITING

MOTION

TRANSPORTATION

OVERPRODUCTION

7 Wastes Observation Worksheet

DEFECTS

INVENTORY

PROCESSING

WAITING

MOTION

TRANSPORTATION

OVERPRODUCTION

7 Wastes Observation Worksheet

DEFECTS

INVENTORY

PROCESSING

WAITING

MOTION

TRANSPORTATION

OVERPRODUCTION

7 Waste Observation Worksheet

DEFECTS

INVENTORY

PROCESSING

WAITING

MOTION

TRANSPORTATION

OVERPRODUCTION

ENNA
KNOWLEDGE INTO PRACTICE

www.enna.com

7 Wastes Observation Worksheet

DEFECTS

INVENTORY

PROCESSING

WAITING

MOTION

TRANSPORTATION

OVERPRODUCTION

KNOWLEDGE INTO PRACTICE

www.enna.com

7 Wastes Observation Worksheet

DEFECTS

INVENTORY

PROCESSING

WAITING

MOTION

TRANSPORTATION

OVERPRODUCTION